Copyright © 2014 by Cynthia Moore
Inner Harmony Books
P.O. Box 16783
Sugarland TX 77496

Editing, Cover Layout and Design by Kitty Y. Williams

Front Cover Images courtesy of
© Can Stock Photo Inc: /marinini, /asado and /christingasner.

Back Cover Images courtesy of
© Can Stock Photo Inc: /marusja, /basel101658 and /WDGPhoto.

ISBN 978-0-9789961-1-6

Printed in the United States of America: First printing

I0086408

About the Author

Cynthia Moore is a Licensed Professional Counselor. She has worked with various populations in the mental health field that include:

- Clinical Director and Coordinator - Residential Treatment - Children, Adolescent. Teen/Young Adults

- Inpatient Hospitalization - Adults, Children and Adolescents

- Partial Hospitalization - Dual Diagnosed Adults with both severe Mental Illness and Chemical Dependency

- Intensive Outpatient Program - Mental Health Adult Intensive Groups

- Lead Clinician - Assertive Community Treatment - Psychosocial

- Rehabilitation Mental Health Outpatient Adult Population

- Practice Manager of two Mental Health Outpatient Clinics

- Care Advocate Behavioral - Utilization Management

- Private Practice

Acknowledgment

Thanks to my Father and Mother who lived a modeled life of commitment and faith to the God they served. Thanks to my mother for her ongoing nurturing of confidence and kind words regarding my abilities. Thanks to my Children who reinforce my faith continuously as they follow the rhythm of their life path.

Table of Contents

FORWARD

INTRODUCTION 5

CHAPTER 1: ODE OF MURKY MUCKY ECHOES 6

CHAPTER 2: RENEWED RESTORED NOTIONS 10

CHAPTER 3: SOUL SAY YES 15

CHAPTER 4: PHILOSOPHY OF MY SOUL 19

CHAPTER 5: DEFINING MOMENT OF MY SOUL 22

CHAPTER 6: THE EPIPHANY 30

CHAPTER 7: THE CONFIDENCE OF GOD 39

Introduction

Over the years along my journey, I have met several individuals who were actually living their life's purpose and not distracted by the lollipops of life. As I interacted with them, I noticed they all presented with an innate knowledge of their contributions to the world. I often wondered how they transcended to such a point in life where they were so confident and peaceful in their existence. Some I knew had very deep spiritual roots and others just seemed like a natural fit to their purpose. As I looked at how they lived their life's purpose with such integrity, and serenity, I began to think about my own existence, and integrity to my purpose in life.

Chapter One
ODE OF MURKY MUCKY ECHOES

One evening I found myself just sitting and reflecting on odes of murky mucky echoes from a time in my life where I used to think I had not made it yet, nor did I fit anywhere in life to include with any group of people. During that time, I did not even feel worthy enough for a healthy relationship of any sort without trauma and drama. I felt so odd and isolated from others. Most of the time, being introverted, I did not mind and was very busy anyway; I could go days without interacting with others. But then there were those moments when I did not feel satisfied with my life, was not using my talents or gifts consistently and had longed to be in a healthy relationship. I was not using my talents because I had not been discovered by the fame God(s) and was valuing the worth of those talents on a financial wealth scale. Now I did not grow up with this notion, because folks around me did not talk about becoming famous; nor did I learn it from television because my father being a preacher did not allow a television in our home. Yet when I moved away from my family and began socializing with others, I incorporated this concept into my stride for success. I would hear others say, they had "finally arrived" or "made it," which they based on being famously known and financially wealthy. So I understood success for the most part as being famously known for talents with a large financial reward. As for having a healthy relationship, I had not met a guy that I synced well with, to include my ex, the father of my children. I just had a hard time meeting a guy with the same values and integrity to sustain a healthy relationship. So I often wondered if others felt the same way. Well, being such an introvert, unless I started hanging out and talking with others, I was not going to find out. So of course, I started listening through casual conversations and found out I was not alone. I heard many people say they felt stuck, all alone or not going anywhere. They mentioned various televisions talk shows they had watched over the years about relationships, careers, and family to learn the right things to do; however at the end of the day they still felt unsatisfied in their relationships and did not fit into any group. Now in my profession of Psychology and as a Licensed Therapist, often times I would hear folks say they were sick and tired of their lives going absolutely nowhere and they did not fit anywhere either. I expected to hear those type of things in therapy sessions. Though I have to be honest with you... At one time in the past, I questioned the whole point of life myself, because at some level it seemed so pointless. Yes, that is exactly what I said. You see there is a myth that Therapists should not have any issues if they are going to counsel others. Is that logical to think that a human would not have any issues in life because of their profession? That would be the same as if I said a Physician should never get sick or a Mechanic's vehicle should never break down. So I will keep it simple: Therapists are human also and humans will always have issues to resolve; it is simply about the ongoing problem solving of any issues that may arise. So yes, this Therapist at one time did not see the value of life. No, I was not suicidal, but I definitely could relate to those individuals who felt they had not gained success or acceptance amongst their peers. When I could not figure out where I belonged, I confined myself to a series of quests, trying to connect to life through love relationships, friends, money (oh lord, tell me about it), exercising trying to get my body in shape and collecting material possessions hoping I would gain some type of fit. Ironically, as I tried to make myself fit into these situations, others involved told me I was out of sync. For example, if I cussed, they reprimanded me for it even though they cussed. It was quite baffling because I really tried to fit in with others on jobs, relationships or friends. So as each attempt to connect failed, I tried to capture as much learning as possible from the experience to help me move forward. I did not want a total loss. But in truth, I was stagnated. You see it is one thing not to fit, but it's definitely another to be stagnated. No matter how I tried to intellectualize the outcome of each experience, I still did not feel a sense of belonging. I could not get the intimate relationship right, friends were acting out, I was not satisfied on my jobs, and always felt lost in the crowd. It was not long before I figured out that I had faulty expectations about my existence, not only with others, but most of all with my life's work. I had not given myself any credit of existence thanks to that old notion of my mediocre income level and my talents not being fame worthy. In spite of the silliness over the income, please let me clarify what I mean when I say fame. I do not mean famous like a Superstar but as in my

8

life's work making a difference on a larger scale. I wanted to be like those folks who were fearless against the Red Sea in front of them and followed their path, ultimately causing changes in the earth. Lord, I was so grandiose. On the other hand, who's to say it will not happen? It has happened in history many times over and over for the good and the bad. Finally I had to talk some sense into myself and balance the scale of my legacy. My age was saying "Honey, get yourself together and get over your delusion of the bigger scale because you are not getting any younger and your talents are for the taking." So each time I alluded to my being as not having made it yet, I validated, violated and restricted my life to a sense of non-existence and feelings of worthlessness. The lack of insight on my distinct purpose hindered me from my true worth and ability to help others as I was designed to do. What is interesting is the times when I presented in my true light, I was very helpful to others who sought assistance from me. Now that I had confronted my ode of murky mucky echoes from the past, it was time to eliminate old messages that interfered with my true destiny to help others.

Chapter Two
RENEWED RESTORED NOTIONS

I am now fifty three years of age and along my journey have met many others who also possessed really unique talents but were not using theirs either, because they too were not famously known with wealthy income. I would rave and talk about how their talents could really benefit the world. Of course, they perceived my opinion as either overly optimistic, idealistic or philosophical. Oh boy, if I could get a dollar for every time I have heard someone say I was philosophical! In many conversations with them, they often mentioned the "someday" concept of being discovered. So wow, they too were waiting on the great Discovery God. I am not beating up on anyone because remember, I too was riding on that very same notion about my talents not being in the public eye and not being received by others with great applause and "Bravos!"

Throughout the course of my journey, I had met many people who carried negative messages about individuals they did not understand in society. Referring to them as crazy, wacky, special, something was wrong with them, or they had problems, the list would go on and on. If someone presented with any spiritual feedback, oh boy, they most definitely had a problem. But looking back on it, I can see they had no awareness of their presentation or lack of insight regarding their own stagnation. They were stagnated in a form of public bullying and abuse toward others due to their own fear of being ridiculed. Now at the time although the comments had not been directed at me, without realizing it, I had processed those comments toward the worth and value of my existence and purpose as if they were credible. Most of the time I was shocked when I would hear such descriptive attacks against others. In spite of being identified by some as a strong female, my self-worth was so low back then that their comments reinforced my failure to express the fullness of my abilities around them, to include any spiritual knowledge obtained from my family of origin. I did not want others to think I was weird, an odd ball or any of the name calling. Now I do want to clarify, those type of comments did not come from my family of origin. Although, I came from a very strict environment, my parents modeled and provided lots of healthy message to my siblings and me. I am not saying they were perfect but they were pretty good; of course as a child I clearly did not think so. Now because I was not getting any younger, I re-evaluated the value of my contributions to the world and realized my talents were positive attributes, not given to me to just have around but for me to share and help others that I encountered along my journey.

So I changed my perception and approached my journey with new notions. The first notion was **to hit the delete button on all negative messages with the quickness and not look back**. I no longer needed to hide behind negative comments made by others as an excuse to not align with my true purpose. I had used those messages for so long as a crutch to stop me from what I thought was making a fool out of myself.

Second, *I told myself I was not in a race or competition against others to complete my journey. After all, it was my life journey and only I was responsible for its completion.* I realized that holding on to those negative comments would eventually tumble me into a pothole; plus racing and competing against others took away my individuality as well as stamina needed to survive my life path.

The third notion was recognizing that *not sharing my talents made my trek burdensome with constant overwhelming feelings of worthlessness.* It always felt so grueling to navigate my daily activities without releasing my gifts. I was not free because I was waiting for the exact fabulous famous moment to share my purpose with the world versus ongoing daily sharing. Interestingly enough, sharing is part of being a good citizen; nevertheless I had totally missed that concept when it came to my talents.

Now on my fourth notion, *I continued to delete and dump any form of rejection and fears about my true value that I had incorporated from the negative messages.* Although my potential may have fallen in the same category as others, I had been afraid to show the uniqueness of my expertise out of fear for being rejected with sneers of not being good enough.

The fifth notion spins off of the fourth notion which was *a real reality awakening. I had allowed so many visions, ideas and concepts that came up years ago in the form of thoughts to just pass me by and on to someone else.* It was as if the vision

12

was there for the taking by whomever was ready. Unfortunately when I would share these visions with others and fail to receive the applause I thought went along with such good ideas, I abandoned them out of fear of ridicule. Years later when I saw those same individuals whom I had shared my ideas with now applauding others who had actualized them, I was so mad at myself for not taking the opportunity. In retrospect, I simply lacked the self-confidence to pursue those visions without the approval of others.

On my sixth notion, *I had to move past all of the should haves of hindsight.* Now it was simply time to, as my Dad would say, "Run and don't look back." So I moved past the idea that others may see me as grandiose, wacky, crazy, overly optimistic, odd and philosophical. That was the moment I became alive on the inside. Yes, I said alive because without the sharing of my talents, my soul was slowly but surely dying. I had been so miserable because I treated my soul and talents the same as a caged bird with the natural capacity to fly, but not released to fly. My ability to connect to others' sensitive issues at their most vulnerable states, or to receive innovative ideas and concepts, was not consistently being shared. Some may view that as ironic for someone who thought their talents were worthy of fame. I know, that is my very point. Now in aligning with my true self, I started hearing the rhythm from my own life path and moved towards it. As I started recovering my sense of purpose and self-worth, I was now able to do a true assessment of my existence

13

and all of the things I had completed so far on my journey. I realized that I had a pretty good track record of hard work and investing my talents with companies where I had worked. However, as with most companies, with respect to their mission, I was not able to express the true essence of my talents in their environment.   In retrospect, I realized that all of my work experiences and relationships whether intimate, friendship, motherhood and or sisterhood had been a preparation juncture to the next level of my life. Life itself had been my teacher, and used all of my collective challenges and experiences as knowledge to help others in need of help along my journey; this brings me to "Soul Say Yes."

Chapter Three
SOUL SAY YES

"Soul Say Yes," is not an effort on my part to convert or challenge anyone's religious belief, personal value system or promote grandiosity. It is my contribution to helping us revive, enrich and surround our lives with an abundance of talents and gifts as we each commit to our sole purpose and life path. The sharing of our gifts is the same wonderful feeling that we now associate with holidays like birthdays, Valentine's, and Christmas. Yes, I know this is a bit optimistic on my part, but if you could just breathe that optimistic notion in for a moment. How refreshing to imagine being surrounded by the constant exchanging of gifts and love. I got the title "Soul Say Yes," from my Dad who was a praying man, Preacher, Pastor and a man with great integrity regarding his commitment to the God he served. When I say commitment, I am not saying he did not have any flaws, but he carried out his life's purpose as a messenger of God with great conviction. My father used to sing the song "Soul Say Yes," in church. (The church organization was Pentecostal; so think of old timey southern Pentecostal services.) Now he had a stuttering speech impediment so I do not remember him saying, "My soul says yes." His stuttering was one of his challenges. Also from what I have been told, my father could not read or write prior to marrying my mother, which was another one of his challenges. My Dad had a little bit more than a 6th grade education. My mother taught him to read and write, proving a great asset to him.

So Dad would lead the audience with a spontaneous "Soul Say Yes," and the members would chime back with "Yes Lord." They would repeat this one chorus over and over while accompanied by drums, cymbals, tambourines and guitar until basically, they were tired. Oh, but let me tell you, sometimes it would go on and on. Talk about meditating; I have had my days of meditations. This modern day talk of meditation has nothing on that old timing Pentecostal service.

Also, I would hear Dad at home, praying and crying out to God, "Soul Say Yes, Lord." I would peep into his room and see him on his knees in worship to God. Sometimes, I could hear him humbly repeating, "Yes Lord," over and over as if he was surrendering himself to the will of God. He would say, "Lord your will be done, not mine, but your will, Lord." Every time, I think about his commitment, it is one of my greatest memories of him. He knew others laughed and made mockery of his speech and lack of education, but it did not stop him. Dad was one of the best Preachers and Teachers I have ever heard in the world of churches. I learned some of my greatest life lessons through his teachings. No, he was neither famously known nor financially wealthy and it did not matter to him that he stuttered. He definitely was not a Preacher who performed dramatic sermons like others who would come through with a boo barge of words as if steering cattle. He was just a humble man with a commitment to his God. He maximized his talents and gifts and ultimately pastored two churches and was a State Bishop over at least twenty one churches in the state we resided. Not bad huh for a 6th grade education?

Now please hang on just a bit longer as I wrap up the origin of "Soul Say Yes." As I continued to review my father's commitment, he put his whole heart, soul and mind into the ministry. He started each service on time and it did not matter if there were two or three members present. He opened every service as if all the pews were full. Whoever was there was going to participate, children and all. So whatever was needed in the service went on. Now folks would wander in late and my Dad never made a fuss about it. However, he never failed to let everyone know the time of the next services. If a member asked him for a ride to church and was not ready upon his arrival, he would send someone else back to pick them up in order to avoid starting services late. The thing that amazed me the most is that he worked a full time job simultaneously while pastoring the two churches. I can still see him when he arrived home from work. He would check on members as needed over the telephone and visit sick members in the hospital. He was such a busy man. Now here is why I wanted you to hang on a bit longer. In my reflection of *his* commitment, I learned the power of commitment. So for my seventh and final notion, I realized that I needed to increase my own commitment to my purpose. In doing so, I had to tell myself some truths. The first truth is people that referred to me as overly optimistic, idealist, and philosophical... were absolutely right. They were also right that I came across as wacky, crazy, and odd because I was not aligned

17

with my true purpose of existence; I appeared out of sync with life. I am no longer ashamed to have those titles associated with me and now hold a unique perspective on life. I made up my mind that if I was going to have any shame, it would be for not following my father's footsteps and staying on the path I had learned as a child. I knew better. I came from a place where folks believed that with God all things were possible; so that is the origin of my optimistic attitude. How else was I supposed to think? We have all heard that children live what they've learned, so why did I allow myself to succumb to public ridicule and deny my true being? After all, the ability to remain optimistic and open to innovative ideas is most definitely a positive attribute to give to others.

Chapter Four
PHILOSOPHY OF MY SOUL

My philosophical perspective is that talents and gifts are not about a few chosen people who get to hog and dominate unique abilities while the rest of us get to stand by in awe and idolize them as superstars. Believe it or not, no matter our social class, we all have arrays of genius to share with each other that come with our birthrights and give us all distinct importance in the communities we serve. Although some of our skills may fall into the same categories, we are each designed with unique abilities for the sole purpose of supporting others along our journey. The support we share is our gift to the world. While I was going through life trying to meet faulty earth bounded validations by seeking renowned fame and financial gain for my purpose, I unknowingly removed myself from sharing the best of who I am with others. I like to visualize all of our talents and gifts as spiritual sunrays to help each other travel through this life as we are confronted and presented with many challenges. As we orbit our paths, pulsating our brilliance, we radiate warm rays of our rhythm and energy that invigorate and strengthen our strides for the endurance of our expedition. The energy helps us not only to complete our journey, but to avoid getting stuck in the toxic P-traps of life. I will talk more about those shortly. The sunrays also help us to transcend and advance from level to level on our paths. I say levels because as we rise above all of our fears and anxieties about our true destinies, we are able to connect to each other in a more humane way and on a larger scale. I used to think other people were doing something beyond the rest of our capabilities when they were recognized as stars and superstars for the work they presented. But I realized they were simply following their life paths and as a result of doing so, were able to bestow possibilities to those that presented with lesser opportunities. Once I understood the value and significance of giving my talents back in the form of gifts to others, I no longer felt as if I did not fit or belong. This notion puts me on a different platform of social interaction.

My path now included following peace with all people by supporting them through my unique artistry. This attitude helped me to help other souls that were dealing with very sensitive and vulnerable issues in their lives and ultimately rekindled their journeys. Now this is not to say we will not encounter uncomfortable feelings of mucky and murky clays along the way. Yes, there are all types of hills, potholes, valleys and obstacles to encounter that will not feel good. However, as I endured and met each stumbling block presented to me, I learned I had achieved another milestone on my mission. Therefore my confidence to encounter any additional challenge to the next level was greater than my confidence prior to the last challenge. I realized all of my hurdles had been the same as on an obstacle course and helped me to improve my confidence for the next challenge. They also connected me to others in a bond stronger than ever, which was the support I needed to push me through to the next stage. I also realized that my most awful and humiliating challenges kept me from becoming complacent in this world or ultimately self-destructing from polluted messages.

Now in order to navigate toward my destination, I needed to free myself to move accordingly to the specifications of the uniqueness of my talents. When I was stagnated, I was trapped in what I refer to as emotional traps of life, just like weighted objects that get stuck in the U-shape of a P-trap underneath most sinks, and tubs. The P-trap connects to another pipe called the S- trap. Without this trap, fuming toxic odors flow back into the house. So when I processed those negative messages, I became trapped from the toxicity of it and ultimately was unhappy and miserable all of the time. I had based my stagnated feelings on my understanding of success and relationships. In truth, I got stuck in an emotional trap of odes because I did not filter out those negative comments. Consequently, it appeared from my perception that some folks were gliding right through life with ease while I was struggling to get from one level to the next. I started out with a boost of sunrays from my family of origin who understood that we were designed to go from level to level and avoid getting stuck here on earth.

Chapter Five
DEFINING MOMENT OF MY SOUL

"Soul Say Yes," helped me to submit and commit to the notion of sharing the best of myself to benefit others along my journey, fame or no fame. Now my interactions with others were intentionally with my authentic existence. When I say I had a boost of sunrays from my family of origin, I really did. It was the most vulnerable part of my journey because it is where my soul started to evolve. So every message from that family counted toward the next level on my life path. The messages helped me to incorporate self-responsibility as I interacted with the various roles in the family. I am referring to the significance of my exchanges with each family member such as Father, Mother, Sister, Brother, Uncle and Aunts. I will visit this in detail later. I remember one of the first healthy messages I heard about me was from my mother when I was around the age of five. One day she was teaching me how to read and write when she leaned over and told me I was a very smart girl; I was so smart that she started me in school early. I remember feeling very good on the inside with the kind tone of her voice and gift of confidence. Her message to me supported my ability to go to school with confidence. As I thought about all of the gunky messages I had collected over the years, I realized I needed to process all messages like a healthy diet that would not do any harm to my life's purpose. I then sought clarity through a mentor to help me filter out messages that had stagnated me and did not belong. Finding a mentor was not an easy task because I

22

needed to make sure they understood my background. I also needed to understand why I had allowed the unhealthy messages to override all of the wonderful healthy messages I had learned as a child. Well it did not take long to resolve that the transition from my family of origin to my independent life path was not a smooth transition as the values from the church that I grew up in were very rigid. So over a period of time, I began adapting to my new environments and slowly but surely did not consistently incorporate my values into my interactions with others. Therefore I had unknowingly authorized negative messages to take precedence over those social exchanges. I soon found myself seeking validation, approval and acceptance from others in the new surroundings.

My mentor diligently worked with and helped me begin filtering out negative messages and I began aligning my soul with my talents. I discovered that I had no other choice but to delete more and more of the messages I had acquired in adulthood which did not fit my role and purpose in life. This deletion period both clarified and helped me to understand my distinct path and I started losing that sense of not fitting or belonging anywhere. It also was not an easy period because as I deleted unhealthy messages, I began presenting as my true self, which threw many people for a loop. They were not prepared for the authentic me. It was not long before I started experiencing very unusual challenges that no doubt defined my soul and made it very clear of my existence and the direction of my path. At the same time, this

23

was one of the most difficult phases in my adult life. The obstacles were so unpleasant that I soon realized the only way out of it was to either abandon my talents and succumb to the challenges, or otherwise completely surrender to my purpose. The challenges lasting about two years were some things in my life which I thought had a sense of security but suddenly had no security at all. Simultaneously, a job, relationship and a couple of friendships unraveled. Once I got through those tribulations, I realized the two year period was a about deception. I found myself in a slew of back to back events where either folks had lied on me or to me. Because all three were unrelated, this coincidence quickly got my undivided attention on the realization that I too had been deceptive in my presentation to others, as I was not aligned with my true being and life's purpose. Without these three events occurring subsequently in my life during the same period, I would not have the confidence, even now, in my ability to share my talents and gifts with others. I tried to endure these battles very privately, but they were so great and beyond my control that others observing me going through them thought my faith and confidence had shaken. Admittedly, I did experience every emotion that goes along with unexpected challenging events, including my health suffering tremendously over one year. I went to at least four Specialists and endured undergoing anesthesia trying to find out what was wrong. I was placed on several medications by each. During one testing period, I recall becoming very angry as needles were being poked repeatedly into my legs to test for nerve damage. I realized that I had absolutely no control over what was happening to me. I hated being sick and no disrespect to my Physician friends or my Physicians, going to a doctor's visit had never been a priority of mine. In spite of my inability to conceal the illness, my value system remained intact and the only thing shaken was the confidence of those individuals who approached me with no faith and confidence. I remember after one person had lied on me at a job, another came to me and said, "I cannot believe you are still here" and that they would have gone home. I had another person say, "I know you will not stick around very long after the way you have been treated." I know they all meant well, but the comments out of their mouths demonstrated fear, lack of faith, courage, confidence, and made it very clear that our coping strategies were from different value systems; one that said "Panic and run" versus mine which said "Stand still and see the deliverance of my God". Yes, I wanted to run many times and not see the faces that spewed so much malice and contention. What kept me from running was one of my values, which said "No weapons formed against me would prosper." So there was no need to process their fears or lack of confidence regarding the outcome of my challenges. There was also no need to run because the source of the lies was true cowardice and by standing on my grounded faith, the enemy would flee". Otherwise I would have faltered on my faith and confidence.

I hung on to my faith and confidence as if it was life or death and strengthened my support system with my mother, children, sister and mentor who were all familiar with my integrities. I checked in with them throughout the two years to ensure I was taking in healthy messages. I was free to open myself up to them for a true assessment of my actions because I knew if I was off task, they would help me get back on task by reminding me of familiar healthy and optimistic messages. Now there were times I just did not get why the same types of challenges kept appearing over and over with no end in sight. It became so obvious that something unusual was happening in my life that demanded a change. Others who did not understand began to say "Wow, there must be something greater for you after all of these encounters." I knew that greater was not about the superficial fame, but it was about me enduring the challenges to the end and being promoted to the next level in this life. During this time, I matured in a way I had never before. I could actually feel the loss of layers as I began interacting with others in a more authentic manner. I was more transparent now than ever because the judgments from others I had once feared, I no longer feared. I strengthened my ability through self-discipline, nurture, support, and maintained a logical sense of order to ensure I was on task to meet my life's goal. I started getting anxiously excited about the good that was coming out of the challenges. Of course I felt the pull and tug to just give up, but the optimistic part of me remained hopeful and reminded me that it gets like that sometimes when we are maturing from one level to the next. My responsibility now was to stand still and stand on my value system.

The origin of my value system was built from many biblical principles learned from my parents when I was a young girl. The bottom line of the principles was about faith, trust, hope and confidence in a God who would give me victory over his enemy no matter what happened in my life. So through the two year period my optimistic side had kicked in. The Philosopher within followed and reminded me of bible stories where God's enemy (who is often referred to as Satan) would try to shake the confidence, faith, hope and trust of many people that believed in God's ability to protect and guide them on their journey. As I pushed through the thickets of conflict with confidence, I knew that no matter what, as long as my deity was on my side I was ok. I remembered reading a story that helped me to finally understand the importance of integrity on my life path and relationship with my deity as I faced adversities in my efforts to meet my life's goal.

The story is pretty simple where God's enemy was going back and forth to the earth walking up and down it; of course looking to bringing misery. So God asked him, had he considered his servant, Job, as there was no other like him. In God's eyes, in spite of all Job's wealth, he was perfect, upstanding in the community, feared him and avoided evil. Ultimately the story tells how God put everything Job owned in his enemy's hands except for Job himself. God's enemy had a belief system that if all of the hedges God had around Job (including his wealth, family and health) were removed, then Job would curse him and no longer maintain the integrity of his sincerity with God. As a human I definitely could relate as I had tried to live my life with faith and hope and still lost relationships and things I had acquired through hard work.

Now Job did not cruise right through these afflictions without feeling the misery that God's enemy wanted him to feel. He initially tried to remain optimistic and said he came into the world with nothing and will leave with nothing, and continued to fear and worship God. But as the hardships kept coming, Job cursed the day he was born, complained, whined about his life and wished that he could die. He expressed his confusion with how God who made him with his hand, could give life and then turn around and destroy him. He felt like God resisted and was against him. Interestingly, in spite of all his misery, when his friends and wife spoke against his integrity to God, Job stepped up and talked about his confidence in the powers and abilities of his God. This story really showed the depth of his relationship with his creator as Job struggled with his internal truth of God's justice, which he could not deny. He simply could not understand his suffering, given he had not violated his integrity with God. So God challenged Job on his abilities by speaking to him from a whirlwind and told him to gird up his loins like a man and answer him to things he had complained about but had no knowledge. God asked him about his whereabouts when He laid the foundation of the earth, when the morning stars sang together and if had he ever commanded the mornings since his days. Now that Job had seen his God, he realized that he had not been abandoned but God had actually shown his confidence in Job's righteousness by authorizing his enemy to take all he had except for him. The story concluded with Job humbling himself with remorse as he acknowledged saying things that he did not understand. Of course as any good story ends, God gave Job more in the end of his time than what he had in the beginning. Over the years, I have heard so many debates about this story where some said God tested Job's faith in Him and others said Job was a pawn between two powers. I disagree with both notions. As a Therapist, one of my interests is genuineness in our interactions with each other. As I carefully read this story, I saw a wide range of genuine emotions and passions displayed by all characters involved, including God. This story was an exemplary illustration for me while in a vulnerable state as a human soul, with no control or understanding of the adversities that I had encountered during the two year period and the willingness to maintain the integrity of my faith with a deity that I had learn of as a child. In spite of what seemed as if the deity was not present, this was the only help that I learned could get me through it; so at the end of the day the story confirmed that the deity had great confidence in the sincerity of my virtue, which ultimately helped me to clarify my true purpose.

.

Chapter Six
THE EPIPHANY

As I moved on to the next level of my journey, the story of Job and his relationship with God and my father's commitment to his life's purpose reinvigorated my soul so much that The Philosopher in me had an epiphany of why my existence started in a family of origin. The family of origin of course is where our physical existence starts with a group of people who help us to develop and prepare for adulthood. In other words, survival and independence. You already know there are various roles in the family to help us with this development. So as I thought about God's role as a protector, authorizer and a creator of his and Job's world, I suddenly got it. I got that the bottom line of coming through my family of origin, was for me to learn how to navigate my life path through incorporating the expectations of each family member role into an independent survival plan of self-responsibility. This removed that old faulty expectation I once had that someone always owed me or was supposed to do something for me. Now of course this concept does not sit well with everyone, especially some traditional thinkers who really have strong beliefs that someone else will take care of them; or those who may feel a sense of entitlement and others are obligated to provide for them as a result of historical events that may have repressed them in some type of way. This concept is not to go against anyone's religious belief system such as some marriages where the man takes care of the woman. It is also not meant to

30

deny anyone's historical cultural experience that may have impacted their ability to progress as successfully as other cultures. But it is about a time in my life where I needed to understand my ability to establish and maintain the integrity of my carved out life path in a manner that was already structured in my best interest, in spite of all the challenges that I had been confronted with in this life. This concept allowed me to grasp something that I understood in order to connect me to my true abilities through an ongoing logical orderly way to successfully meet my life's goal through self-discipline, nurture and support as I continued to transcend from level to level in the absence of my family of origin. Yes, I say level to level because I believe that my soul transcended through conception to my family of origin, to my life's purpose and then will pass on to the next life, which is the next level. When the appointed time comes and all is unveiled, I will clearly see and understand all. So please allow me to ease you into this concept a little bit closer when it comes to managing our life's purpose. This may get a little sensitive because I do need to touch on those vulnerable areas in our lives where we have been socialized to work against our personal goals and stride.

When I looked at the role of my father in our family being the protector, authorizer and provider for us, I remember how he carved out a way for us to survive. If he had not, he would have been considered a sorry fellow, which nowadays it is called a deadbeat. Anyone who came to our house for visits had to get his authorization, which was reinforced by my mother in his absence, otherwise, they were considered as intruders. Incorporating the characteristics of The Father's role into self-responsibility for my life path meant deleting old notions about not only who was going to provide for me but who and what I was going to authorize in my life. I had been raised in a time where for the most part the girls outside of my home talked about marrying the man on a white horse who would sweep them off their feet and take them away from their father's castle to his own. As a young girl, it was all silly talk and made absolutely no sense. Besides that, I never heard my father or mother say such things to me or my siblings and they had three sons and seven girls. But of course the farther I moved from my family values, I adopted such a concept. I clearly saw my parents as helpmates to each other where they each contributed to the purpose of their union while simultaneously modeled a sense of independence to their individualized purposes in life. Now I started my adult life very independently following this path, hoping to join with a husband as a partner for a joint mission, all while maintaining my life's purpose. However, once married I was soon side tracked with the idea of being a wife and mother with my husband being the sole provider. This was not unusual during the eighties and nineties. Although this may have blended into the fabric of marriages during that time, it was not long before the light of my soul slowly but surely began withering away and I just did not feel complete on the inside. Now I want to speak clearly here. I thoroughly enjoyed being a mother and my children have always been the joy in my life. But as my husband excelled in his military career receiving all of his promotions and awards, I felt as if a part of me had been dismissed. No, I was not jealous, I just did not feel a sense of continual growth as he was growing. In retrospect, I would whine and cry on the inside with faulty expectations from my husband to fill in the gaps, but he could not and did not have a clue what I needed. We were young and clueless. Ultimately, there were other challenges in the marriage that took a toll on me where after many years of trying to live through it, I removed myself from the marriage to regain and restore peace in my mind.

Now that I was single, it became very clear what had been missing. I slowly but surely had abandoned the person I once knew. Of course the details are too much to tell right now but over a course of time, my faith began to dwindle after several attempts of trying to incorporate the helpmate union concept that I had witnessed from my parents' example. However, I had partnered with a husband who had not witnessed such a union, thus his best efforts to emulate one failed as underlying issues from his own family of origin interfered with the ability to do so. Being single meant that I was responsible for my survival so I merged the characteristics of The Father's role into personal responsibility. Doing so eliminated the blame game and it held me personally accountable, which quickly eliminated any whining, crying, complaining and blaming others when things did not go the way I had hoped. This included my career as well as relationships, whether intimate, family or friends. As a single woman, I had to learn that taking the role of The Father in my life meant putting hedges up in such a way that I only authorized what I really desired in my life, which was not foolishness and games. Now this was not easy and even to this day in spite of all the discipline I had as a young girl, I still struggle with resisting authorizing things in my life that go against the integrity of my value system. There are those times when my flesh wants what it wants whether it goes against my health, diet or if it is a fellow that I really like who may call and want to tap on my door late at night. I still struggle with not answering the phone, especially if the brother has goods. I have to always remind myself through the characteristics of The Father that he is no good for me when it comes to my integrity, in spite of his goods. I learned that if I wanted respect in my life, whether that of a job or any relationship, I had to discipline myself with self-control and not compromise my values over inflated fears such as being alone or unable to provide for myself; otherwise I would be compromising my protection. As I continued to commit to my true purpose, the delete button went full force and relationships of all sorts without integrity unraveled. This did not mean that I did not interact with those folks, I simply no longer allowed the same access to me as I had in the past. What is interesting about the whole thing, is that they were not bothered by this one bit, they just simply dialed the next number. Of course they all have come back from time to time to see if they can re-gain access. Access Denied, because Daddy was home and in charge now. In the past I had opened and re-opened those doors many times because I was caught up in the social concept of

34

being single meant being alone; but I now know that was a dead end street not going anywhere and of course a stagnated situation wondering why I was not meeting the right man in my life. I had to get in the lane of integrity and renew my notions about my true desires in a relationship. When I hear people talk about what women or men do wrong in relationships, I feel what matters is that they understand the purpose of their existence and authorize others into their life according to their purpose. In the past, I met several guys that had good standing in the community but behind closed doors they clearly lacked social graces and honor. Without the characteristics of The Father's role, I had unknowingly authorized these intruders into my life based on their sweet talk. I used to feel so good when a man would ask me where I had been all of his life, or wished he had known me when I was younger. Sure at the time it sounded good and I thought they were really saying something wonderful to me. After all, I had been socialized that a great guy will come along and say wonderful things to me if he was interested and then provide a great life for me. Still their behaviors that followed showed me they did not have a clue of the design for my life and furthermore, no interest in a partnership with me. I remember all the crying days of thinking no one will love me in my actuality because I was only good enough when they were younger. At the time, I took this feedback as rejection, but I now clearly get that our principles were so far apart that it would not have been in the best interest of my life's purpose.

As I adopted the role of The Mother into self-responsibilities, the nurturing helped me to connect to the purpose of my being by giving me insight that I had the ability to nurture my talents to maturity and I alone was responsible for the development and progress, the same as if the talents were my children. Often times I have heard others refer to a project or the initiative of a business as their baby. It all started to make so much sense and was so simple. With this concept, I felt quite empowered and my self-esteem was invigorated to move forward and not abandon my life responsibilities with one excuse after the other. Previously, I had always relied on others to tell me when I was ready or good enough. This time The Nurturer ensured and provided me with the confidence that I already had everything inside of me to maximize my existence and was ready to proceed to the next level. This is what I love about The Nurturer: it knows my value, my worth and promotes me where I am in spite of others' opinions, doubts and negative messages. With constant positive reassurance from The Nurturer, I am able to stay out of the emotional P-traps of life and move forward on my path without two left shoes, while still ensuring my best interest.

Now as I incorporated The Sister's role, I reflected on the relationship with my six sisters who reinforced the self-nurturing responsibility in the absence of my mother. They were one year to thirteen years my senior in age, so I absolutely could not get this wrong. The characteristics I learned from this bunch ranged from comforting me when I cried to sharing their secrets with me.

This fortified the integrity of a confidant and supporter not only to myself, but to others who shared their deepest pains, sorrows, and regrets. I should have guess then that being a Therapist was on my life path with all the secrecy my sisters bestowed on me. I remember when I was in the sixth grade, a boy who was a friend of mine told me we had to break up because his mother told him he could only have one girlfriend. When he told me, my first reaction was shocked because I did not know we were boyfriend and girlfriend. My second reaction was I cried so hard that one of my sisters reached out to comfort me and it felt so good that someone understood my hurt. Along this journey I had heard many folks refer to their sister as their best friend who always had their back; it became clear that I needed to become my biggest supporter and cheerleader.

Now my brothers were very logical in their approach to life and from my interactions with them, I learned I needed to logically approach not only relationships but decisions in every other area of my life.

In reflecting on all of the self-accountability characteristics merging together on my behalf to help me maximize my purpose, for a short moment I was left in a state of flux, because it did not take long to realize my work was cut out for me. You see it was one thing to delete those old messages and poor socialized ideas, but it sure was another thing to incorporate this self-responsibility philosophy into my life. The picture was clear that in the past, I had approached my existence all wrong with two left shoes. I had missed the point that I was totally responsible not only for what I authorized into my life, but for the protection, nurturing, and supporting of my talents, which meant the destiny of my soul. Now, this did not mean I would not have any supporters, but that my introverted personality needed a little dose of assertiveness and I could no longer blame anything or anyone on where I belonged in life or fit. I could not blame a man when I did not get what I desired in a relationship. Nor could I blame friends who lacked integrity in friendship. I also could not blame supervisors for not promoting me in a company. Oh, I was no longer fond of the epiphany, it was a great philosophy but to actualize it meant transcending responsibility. It seemed easier in the past to hold all others accountable for my stagnation and simply not move forward and just become complacent until the end of my time. My misery suddenly looked just fine and not so bad after all. Yet it was that peaceful existence that I had witnessed of others who were actualizing their life's purpose that kept nagging at me about my true existence in the absence of incorporating self-responsibility. Although the philosophy made perfectly good sense to me and I could see how to apply this in so many areas of my life, I still had stiffness of fear regarding taking full charge of my life, which brings me to "The Confidence of God".

Chapter Seven
THE CONFIDENCE OF GOD

I mustered up courage and girded up my loins as a woman who truly believed in the power of committee, confidence, authority and integrity and pledged my existence and talents to a life-long commitment of my Soul Say Yes. I was no longer living a life of deception like those who had lied on or to me during the challenging years. The messages that once hailed shady attacks, subjected and exposed me to a life full of self-doubt and second class citizenship not only in my natural but spiritual life was now out of earshot and eliminated. That old citizenship devalued my intelligence and capabilities as a leader, woman, female, wife and mother. It did not respect my voice nor gifts from my design. The second class citizenship was not my God given birth right. I was designed through a value system with spiritual leaders and departing from that notion had only jeopardized my existence (my soul) which was designed to live forever; I would not live forever in misery as a second class citizen even beyond this life.

Now that I had accepted my purpose in all of its worth, The Trailblazer in me was ready to lead, inspire, encourage and innovate through motivation. The Woman in me had taken her position in life as a female who now understood her significance and how to nurture vulnerable and sensitive issues; the same as a mother to an evolving child. As far as The Wife in me, I restored the hedges of honor and authorization was now only for a man of integrity and compatible value system. I was finally walking in the

39

rhythm of my path like my father who walked confidently in his path and not the social standard templates of life. The path he walked was modeled after the confidence of God.

Through the two year challenges, I realized I had to walk this same path of faith which was very simple. I even had someone during this time to remind me that I was a woman of faith. I recognized that in the past, I had missed the simplicity of God's confidence in my life so many times. This became even more evident to me through an event where I received a call from my house alarm monitoring company to alert me that the alarm had gone off. Given that I was not expecting anyone, we agreed to call the local police department. I arrived home prior to the police arrival, got out of my car and perused the external property for intrusion. I returned to my vehicle and patiently waited for police assistance. The police arrived and checked the property the same as I had and confirmed no external intrusion. He then instructed me to open the door so he could confirm no intrusion was on the inside of the house. Well that made sense. So I unlocked the door and stepped forward to go inside. I then heard a very quiet voice from the officer who said, "Ma'am, I am going to go in first; I need to make sure the place is safe." As soon as I heard his voice say he needed to go first, I suddenly had an epiphany that the officer had spoken confidence and placed his life on the line to protect me the same way God would do for us. When I first stepped forward, I had not considered the possibility of any danger. It took that very second of him saying it before I got a clue that if indeed there had been an intruder, he was there to protect and shield me from danger. Thank God the officer had confidence in his ability and knew he needed to make sure the inside property was safe to enter.

I was so used to being single and handling things that I forgot his purpose, the same as I often did with God with sudden unexpected challenges and those things in my life which I had no control over. I then remembered many occasions when I had not waited for God to go in first to shield and protect me. I had been too anxious and thought I could handle matters myself. But I had to learn to let God show off his abilities and step back and let him go in first as my rock and fortress to protect and shield me when others attempted to intrude and overtake me. Better yet, he has assured me through scriptures that when I walk through valleys and shadow of death, I do not have to fear any evil because he, the confident, one is with me.

Honing in on this confidence was reinvigorating to my soul as it restored faith that I was not alone through the most difficult challenges I may encounter on my journey.

During this same timeframe when my alarm went off unexpectedly, I was going through a very vulnerable period in my life. I opened my wallet one day and realized my driver's license and social security card were both gone. I wondered if I had changed purses and simply forgot to remove it, but I remembered using both since the purse change. I was so baffled at being unable to find those items. I called on a friend who calmed me

41

and took the time to carry me to the necessary agencies to quickly replace both items.

Shortly afterwards about a week later while trying to get to a physician's appointment, I suddenly found myself experiencing the inability to speak normally and had difficulty breathing. I called my daughter hoping she was still up from her third shift duties and would answer; thank God she did and called 911. The next thing I remembered was an emergency room nurse firmly giving me directions to follow. I had the most difficult time coordinating his directions but ultimately was able to do so. I had apparently experienced complex complications from severe chronic migraines. The nurses and physician informed me that the symptoms were presenting like a small stroke known as Transient Ischemic Attack, TIA. I was kept over a couple of days for observation to rule out the TIA. I quickly recovered to my normal functioning and was discharged so I thought things should calm down. No, not the case. A few days later I received a phone call from my bank informing me that my account had been compromised and cloned and I needed to have my debit card replaced. A week later I discovered that another item was missing from my purse. It reminded me of the 911 emergency where I realized I was on an emergency table surrounded by medical staff; my clothes were off and my breasts and fat belly were fully exposed. I thought for sure, "Girl, you will not meet your husband here." I felt embarrassed, vulnerable and wanted to jump up and leave but was still too disoriented and confused to do so. I realized no matter how I did not like the vulnerability and exposure, it was time to let go and have confidence that I was being well taken care of by the healthcare professionals. At that point, I remember my body collapsing backwards in a totally relaxed manner.

As I surrendered and began to place my confidence in the integrity of the relationship between myself and the God I served, my recovery started at that moment. I did not like the firm rigid voice and strong hands of the nurse, yet the more I followed his firm instructions the more I recovered. I remembered tearing up and crying for a few minutes when I first heard the nurses tell me they were trying to rule out a mini stroke that could lead to a major stroke. When I realized what was happening, the tears and frustration stopped and it felt as if I needed to do everything they told me in order to get better. There was no time for a pity party because the nurse who guided me was guiding me with conviction in his ability to help me recover. So why lay and pity myself when the nurse and other medical team members worked so vigorously and in such great assertiveness to get me up and back on my feet. Finally I felt invigorated and ready to carry on and finish my journey. When I became fully alert and oriented, I thought about God's confidence in my ability to complete my journey as he reminded me through scriptures that the race is not given to the strong and swift but to the one who endures the journey until the end.

Now that I know this journey is about the integrity of my commitment to the purpose of my existence as well as to the God I serve, I am able to navigate my journey with authority. It was the relationship between Job and God that got my attention and the value of his integrity in their relationship. As I focused on God's confidence where he took claim of the creation of the earth, I thought who can argue with such a being that takes and lays claim on the universe's formation? Talk about confidence. If I talked in this manner folks would say I had lost my mind, was conceited and outright crazy.

The truth is, we have all seen the moon and stars and we know we did not put them there. We woke up to the very existence of the moon and stars. So God walking in his bold existence took credit and responsibility and told us he spoke light and darkness into actuality and separated the day from night. So I finally understood the relationships between the roles of self-responsibility in relation to my talents and my need to incorporate the confidence of God which was simple.

He first spoke confidence of his abilities into existence. Secondly, he placed hedges of protection around his creations. He had done this on more than one occasion, such as with Adam in the Garden of Eve and again with Job. Thirdly, he only authorized access to his creations based on integrity. I now knew I had to take and lay claims by speaking my talents and desires into existence, protecting them and only authorizing those with integrity to participate so that the integrity of my purpose was not compromised.

Now that I started following the blueprint of my distinct purpose, I removed the barriers that were once allowed to interfere with it. I began calling my accomplishments into existence with timelines and placed hedges of protection around them, only granting access to individuals of integrity. Finally, I committed a minimum of one hour a week towards the formation and actualization of my endeavors, the same as my father showed up for church every week and started service on time as if all the pews were full. Ultimately as I allowed my soul to walk the rhythm of its own path, my talents began to make room for me and others began radiating their brilliance as support to my efforts. Their collective gifts of warm energetic rays of rhythm increased my confidence to hone in and submit to my unique design. I surrender to my mission. Soul Say Yes.